1

be the
blooming flower

freya ede

take the hand

my words open to you

guiding you through

the journey

of new beginnings

take these words

as your own

paint the world you hold

in those hands

call it *mine*

as you deem yourself

restored

rebuilt

take my words

stretch them to the emptiness

soon to be filled

with the newfound peace

-my heart to yours

the sun rose

to the tears spilling down my face

this is my voice

these words saved me

from the safety that was once broken

-poetry heals

contents

for when you are buried deep

the wall

times where

the wall between you and me,

stands invisible

immensely tall.

i could spend days

just trying to chip it away.

the hole is there,

but you remain to fill it in.

refusing to see the work i had just put in

cycle.

numb

no.

i'm numb,
not sad, not happy
not fine.

when you give them your all
you often don't get it back.
it leaves you empty

no.

numb.

the words i need

haven't been spoken

for so long

that my mind which bleeds

hasn't yet been sown up

by the reassurance

needed to save me.

-overthinking

the words i read

as that young girl

have taught me that kindness

grows old

in those who are still so young.

holding it in

through a thin glass pane

waiting for it to shatter

the touch of it on my skin,

i had felt it break

again, and again.

once its fixed

its destined to fall

with time.

-stitches

carried weight

sometimes the pain

we inflict on ourselves

is really

the pain

most caused by others.

the happiness no longer lingers

like the old shoes i once wore

sat at the back door

-unwearable

failure to myself

i could tell myself

you mean everything
with the world in your hands.
you are the most beautiful,
comfortable around her
you are good enough,
knowing the knowledge of a lifetime.

some days i do,
feel them things
but the fear of failure always,
always sinks in.
the words spilling out of their mouths
bury me deep

until i can't dig anymore.

why does the world

turn-pointing at me

when the forests burn

deep into the evergreen of the earth

i am only the flint

who lights the flames

for the rest of them to pat down

-rage

she was always too much for someone.

she was wrong,
she had given her all to you
every little thing you wanted.
exceeded.

she was always left wondering what she did wrong
the answer?

nothing
it was all you
you were blind.

i feel confined

with the crowds

in the space i keep empty

-headspace

time is deadly

when it's trapping you with the thing you hate the
most

with the demons that break you

a massacre of silent cries

crammed into the biggest room

with the door

at the centre of my heart

time is deadly

when the waves cut and crash

in a place you belong,

a place you were meant to swim

why is my body the punching bag?

the trees grow

for a lifetime

they are cut down

by those with hearts

either shattered from a broken past

or stemmed from a selfish soul

the news shattered me

my heat splitting into

two.

she wanted to uncover the marks

raw with guilt,

fresh with uncertainty.

it was those marks which were

clean for so long.

it was those marks which were

torn up, into new ones.

i have been told

that to be anxious

before entering the doors

of a space that confines you

is to be a baby

in a place

you thought you were

mature

my heart is breaking

-a million pieces

oh, how i wish to be the moon

surrounded by darkness

in a world illuminating through

the flames of our own anger

-the moon is safe

i feel like i'm drifting,

away from everything that matters

everything important

i don't have the energy to catch myself

like i always did.

but what do they expect me to do

when no help is offered?

carry on falling

until i hit the ground?

my past had buried me

beneath the soil

of my own skin

the only way to escape

was to claw my way free

don't push me below

the line

for feeling overwhelmed

within my own thoughts

the voices proceed to claw their way through

no matter how

strict

degrading

angry

you present your feelings to be.

-my anxiety is not punishable

breaking into a million pieces

makes the numbest people

feel the best pain

when you feel nothing

self-destruction

reminds the mind

that it's still alive

-pain is the cure

her body was thrown

into a pool of arms

sworn to keep her safe

when the hands let her fall

she plummeted

into the arms of her own

pain

-pain is safety

my mind feels this kind of pain

that has begun to make me question

the skin i choose to saw open

my mind makes me feel the kind of hurt

that has begun to make me stretch

my skin across

nails on wooden board

to examine the twisted body

i am imprisoned in

-am i worth it?

when they leave

they leave you broken

after the agony

they used to cause

when that broken soul

had nothing but that

attention

they decide to love themselves

in the most

evil way

they can

-self inflicted

i had held up my weapon

far into the absence of dawn.

horizons away

the only anguish i ever knew

was the breaking of my skin.

it remains.

drawn to the aurora

closest to my sphere

-the horizon attracts me

lately,

the face i see in the mirror

is disfigured beyond belief

with my eyes pointing into the direction

of that someone i used to be

they showed me

my voice was

hollow

by digging

into my heart

when you feel the water

boiling over the pot,

your legs tingle

as if they are about to be doused

with boiling water

and your brain becomes fogged

frozen in time

as it takes every ounce of strength

to subside the wave of water

from reaching the point

of destruction

-panic

i am convincing

myself

i am supposed to arm myself

with blades

as i was taught to use them

as self defence

-threat

the words that were promised to you

on that dreary day

danced through the streams

-right into the ditch

he knifed my body

into the ground

and expected me to rise

as well as the

morning lit sun

how can you tear me apart?

for being the girl, you raised

for me to change

and be shredded

the second time i birthed my new soul

-changing for your words

oh, the pain

feels so good,

relieving the duty that you

always did wrong

-guilt

the ups and

       d

        o

         w

          n

          s

of my rollercoaster

bring change

creating friction between the tracks

of my mind, and my clarity

-everyone sees it except me

for when love plants its seed

once you have her,

don't let her go

you'll know when.

a dot from space

means a million stars to you

if i had known that was the last time

i would have hugged you

that little bit tighter

the day is bright

yet you aren't here

your last shadows

shield the light i hold

from the memories

flickering by

like a string of roll film

lit up in my head

-just a memory

the arms that once wrapped around me

keeping me safe

when i felt darkness

were always meant to be

curled around someone

who feels safety

within their own skin

-too much to hold

i always left

i was scared,

scared of losing something i was attached too.

but something changed.

i let my heart take over

i let it win

and now she is mine.

hearts

as my heart reaches out for hers,

her heart calls for mine

the unity of our love

freely entwined

as one

you had pushed me so far under

the morals that i once held

i have been trying to find the love my heart

once had ever since

i once called love

being next to them

in the worst way imaginable

i once called love

toxicity

in hopes i was the one

who was the devastator

-love is deceiving

you painted me

with your fantasies

and hoped

i would see them too.

how do i comprehend

that the words given from you

to me

aren't lies

just like the rest of them.

you are the tape

holding them together

after they just ripped you off

you thought you could stick

it all back together

when you were the one torn apart

in the first place

-hold together your own love, its much more
important

the space feels crowded

empty boxes,

lined walls

it's for the best she said

i never felt so free

until i walked away.

you pushed my body into the sea

and then

you dived into the depths of the ocean

to bring my breathe

right back to the surface again

-manipulation

i sit here

where old memories thrive

that silky touch that once was

holds me close

in the abyss

i sit here

wondering when i'll see you next

that gentle hand

sweeping my neck away

reminiscing of the touch

that once crashed

at me.

as a wave

the words you spoke to me

healed my wounds

on their journey

to becoming long lost

scars.

her touch

sealed the line

of trust

from my heart

to hers.

-leap of faith

how does leaving

the only heart

you had ever loved

not say

inconvenience

when the time i spent loving

was a waste.

your lips

dance with mine

to make the sweetest music

you have ever tasted

time is empty

when it comes to love

if they are *yours*

yours would be a lifetime

that is the thing

about love

it fills your body

until they are within everything

you do

moments like these

i ache to wrap

wrap my intelligence

round that sour taste

of yours

-double sidedness of love

you had shaken me

until the pieces fell apart

and i was no longer

whole

come back

but,

the days would grow longer

as id pluck the stars out the sky

to re-light

the heart you turn into ashes

-they keep me safe in the darkness

why should the weapons

used against you

be pointed

at the smooth side of my skin

-i gave you what you wanted

the sweetness of my heart

ignored the salt you

drenched me in

a person who excites you

in a way that makes you soar freely

is a person

worth waiting for

-soulmates

do not patronise me

i cared

but sometimes the love

you give to them

is better off

given to the only one

that was ever present

i am scraping

the tar

that you stuck

to my skin

in hopes of pleasing

me with pain

no.

is not yes.

-consent

my love

i know you have been

cut

by those that

once watered you

the ones singing

to you

are the ones

praying that you grow

-not all the same

the sweetest honey

poured from the mouth of the one i loved

covered the skin i cherished

yet did i know

the honey would never turn sour

no matter the acid they poured in

-the guilt caused by your honey

for when you want to flourish

honey,

your life is moving

through this life

take the hand of the memories you made

you may not be able to let go

but carry it along

on your new pathway through living

-you are not defined by them

once the glass has shattered

only time will give you clarity

a clear vision,

through your new pane

fresh and unbroken.

marks upon my skin

they scream, damaged

a broken past

only my own body knows

when it is ready to heal.

only i will know when i have done it.

-bloomed

in that second

it seems like the release

of a lifetime.

in that lifetime

it's no release at all.

the days you live

after their shadow is gone

are your days to thrive

in a world full of heartbreak

and ache.

one rainy day

will soon turn into the brightest of all.

-don't hold onto the darkness

know that

the earth around you

sleeps peacefully

when your heart breaks silently in the night

know that

the earth around you

still flourishes

even when you refuse to water it

the earth will mature

even when you pour every

litre of doubt

into your hollow heart.

-it grows despite the doubt

being honest

can sometimes reveal true colours.

the real consequences

they are craving to feed it,

our guilt.

sometimes we need to keep our true selves

to ourselves

only then will we feel free

for they will never understand

-independence

have no expectations

build only out of what your brain does not know yet

be free.

take the anxieties weighing you down

by the ankles

and stand up tall

to get to the side of your mind

that feels free

from what was once holding

you back from achieving the goals you set out

for the best version of you.

-you are at the other side

sometimes the days

which have the darkest end

are the days which

show you those with the lightest beginning

-clarity

the new mistakes teach you

why the old ones went wrong

the importance of other people's lives

only means little

when your life is deemed by itself.

your kindness has more potential to heal yourself

when you need it most

than someone else who barely needs it at all.

-coming first

trying to outshine me

is like trying

devastate

mother nature's sun

that morning glory flower

opens for the golden light

putting on a show

upon my windowsill.

until the light falls

and moon appears

that bud cascades

onto the destiny of the day

and a new one arises to face barricades

in such elegance and faith

all over again.

-fall to rise.

my hands

were the perforators

of my pain

i am a mirror

if i hurt myself

i will only find those

who hurt me too.

-heal yourself

letting go of the debris

that once covered you,

sets you on a path

free from the weight

that was pinning you down.

people take no notice

of the strength

and courage

it takes to turn up

to a place

your body urges to run from

in a matter of seconds

before exploding

-anxious days

my beauty is not defined

by what you call *wrong*

my beauty is pain

driven from the depths of

the emptiness i had felt.

my beauty is not the marks on my skin

damaged by the hands of someone

lost in a broken world.

my beauty is what i've overcome

through this cruel recovery

my beauty is more than what i show.

its who i've become

on this road.

-driving

hush honey

the world is yours to breathe.

take the hands you own

make your own art

in the world where you feel alone.

no more doodles across your skin

only the ink of nature

creating the pages

of this world you now hold.

-the new path of life awaits

the words from my pain

have set me free.

when i can let myself go

in this book

completely

i will have forgiven

the words given to me

which once

broke me.

sometimes the most delicate poems

give the most reason.

-simple

as time moves on

the fear of living begins,

begins to subside

among the ever-growing shrubs

intertwined through your heart

as time moves on

the earth below your feet gets wiser,

wise enough to teach you

within the transcending shards

distressing your skin

as time moves on

the air shares natures medicine,

medicine to become clear

within the torridness

seeping through your tears

-moving on, forgetting the pain

the infinite span

of the world's existence

is just enough to find ourselves

pieced together

by our own love.

-healing through time is a process

you are a bud

with a thousand glances

but not worthy

of them

captivating your upcoming

bloom

-trust where you are

my wilting foliage

dwindles, diminishes

through the wind

my sickly stem

branches, bowed

into the gleam

of the newly birthed sun

-grow through the darkness

before you go spreading your heart out,

like daisies

know that there are thorns

destined to pierce through your delicate barricade.

-daisy chain

the future

is miles away

take the pain that burns you now

turn it into knowledge to guide you on a path

to the peace that life will hand you

when you are ready

trim the leaves back

to see even more life

push right through

-stronger

for when you have bloomed

flowers are temporary

so is pain.

bloom in the elegance of life

knowing next time

will be the same

-future you is blooming

find yourself gazing

into those eyes of yours

understanding they still shine

from seeing true love

-you

why is it that you find yourself

feeding those which starved you

and cooking for those

who fed you

when you could not find the strength

to spoon feed your own diminishing self.

-giving back to those who saved a life

find yourself

longing to see the body it sees now

and say *thankyou*

humanity

is standing up

for those who live without a voice

and by taking away their inhibition

you find the reason behind

your souls' true purpose.

i am so proud

of the hurdles you have jumped

to reach this line,

the place you call finished.

but the place i see as

the start of the life

you craved ever since

you had started running away.

you are the rising sun

radiating the ingredients

for the earths bloom

-*i am blooming*

find your hands touching those

who have never felt

the sensation of someone

who ever cared

-selflessness

breathe.

with the rhythm of the waves

as if you were the sand

falling within the pattern

of the moon and suns balance

your heart is now tender,

tender with your own love

take your peace

allow it to touch your heart

as if it was healing it

all over again

-healing is infinite

take the sun and stars and sprinkle them out where we all can see. let us captivate your beauty and creation you have put in place. let us see the work you had once put in and let us see the result of someone who uses the most dangerous things to make the most magnificent scene. let us admire you for your hard-driven journey. let us glare at the sky you have re-lit with your power and strength.

let them promises

attached to your petals

wilt away.

let your own expectations grow through

more constant, more honourable

than the last

-trust yourself.

the avocado tree has waited your lifetime

to see you bloom

can't you see

it been waiting its whole lifetime

to bloom too.

-celebrate

be gentle

with them hands others are meant to hold.

take them both

intertwine them into each other

your touch is enough

to teach you everything you need to know

about yourself

-listen to your body

a heart that loves

is a heart that

gets given a life worth living for

it was on that day

where you found your ground

the sun whispered to the moon

she is her own light

let her spread the wisdom she now holds

and allow the ground below her newly found feet

to flourish.

she no longer needs me.

if my words to you

have meant nothing

why are you in awe

of the life you now get to live

my heart codes the sequence

to that kind of peace

you find within the days you can

call yourself *home*

-self-love

my finertips soar

against them metal gates

creating a sound to make my soul giggle

although my body was growing old

i yern to feel young

in them soft fingers of mine

feeling the world for the very first time

-born again

poetry saves those

who are too wise to live

with their mind

not poured out to the world around them

-let it go on paper

find your strength

in the things that separate you

from the rest of humanity

-unique

love those

who lack empathy

be that girl

you once saw as a princess

through them eyes of yours

thank you for finding my heart on these pages and soaking it all in. thank you for listening to the pain in which i have felt, and which i have scattered across this book. you are not alone through this journey to health and peace. you will get there; time will heal you. thank you for accepting the world around you for the way it is and for finding it in yourself to purchase the words that may just push you to that place you need to be. be kind to yourself, be kind to others. you are beauty in the purest form. thank you.

-a letter from someone who cares

this is not the end